Push and Pull

By Leslie Garrett

Contents

We push and pull when we play.

Push to Play

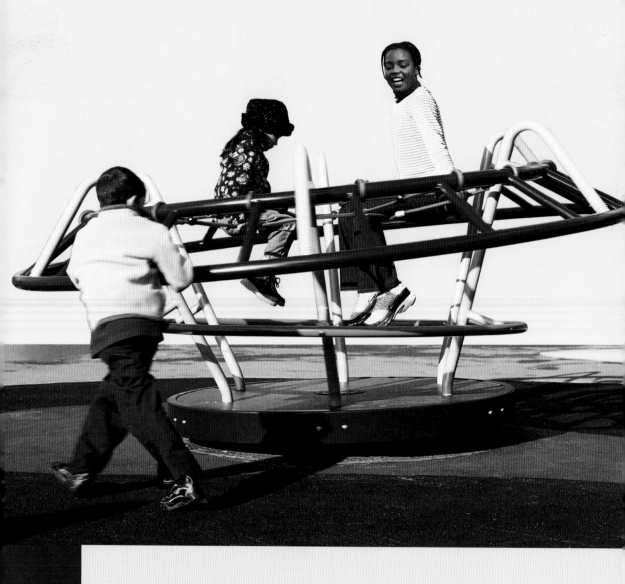

Push the merry-go-round
to make it spin.

Push the swing to make
it go up in the air.

Pull to Play

Pull the rope to move
the ribbon closer.

Pull the cart to make
it go forward.

Push and Pull to Play

Push to Play

Pull to Play

Pushing and pulling helps us play!